WHAT PEOPLE ARE SAYIN(

"For the past 20 years, Bill Garner has been on the cutting edge of life sciences innovation. His book recounts the gritty and at times disheartening tale of what it is like to be a biotech entrepreneur. Through it all his energy, inspiration and optimism triumph as he works in perhaps the most complex and dynamic economic sector in America today. Along with books like *Gene Dreams, The Billion Dollar Molecule, The Cell Game* and *The $800 Million Dollar Pill*, I plan to recommend it to anyone thinking of getting into biotech."

—JAMES KUO, MD, MBA, CHAIRMAN OF MSK PHARMA

"Anyone who has already or is currently thinking about taking a drug from the lab to the market should read *Garnering Capital*. The author's story, rooted in pragmatism and spiced with ideals, will provide insight to help you better understand the progression of capital strategies, protection of an asset (IP), and realization of your drug or product's potential. Hopefully this will become a part of the "must read" list for students interested in the world of bioscience business."

—JAMES B. LAUFENBERG, CO-FOUNDER, PRESIDENT AND CEO, IMMUNOGENETIX THERAPEUTICS, INC., AND FORMER EXECUTIVE AT MARION LABORATORIES.

"Struggling to survive the fundraising process with your soul intact? This is the book to take on the perilous journey. Kudos, Bill, for your remarkable candor, advice, and humor in the face of unending trials by fire! I will recommend this to every CEO and other road warrior I know."

—ROBERT WATKINS, CEO, GLOBAL RECRUITMENT FIRM RJ WATKINS & CO.

"This important new book gives us a firsthand look at the inherent challenges of converting ideas into marketable products, and provides innovators and investors with vital key insights for successful collaboration."

—DENNIS H. PENN, PHARM.D., MBA, PRESIDENT & CEO, MASTCELL

"As an investor relations advisory company we wish all of our clients would read this book. It is an outstanding roadmap for entrepreneurs."

—KEVIN FICKLE, PRESIDENT, NUWA GROUP LLC

GARNERING CAPITAL

MAKE THE RIGHT DECISIONS.
PENETRATE THE MARKET.
ACHIEVE PROFITABILITY.

WILLIAM J. GARNER, MD, MPH

www.egbadvisors.com
@InnovationMD on Twitter
www.innovationangelcard.org

Published in the United States by
New Voices Press
315 W. 70th Street Suite 6C
New York NY 10023
212-580-8833
info@katzcreative.com

Library of Congress Cataloguing-in-Publication Data

William J. Garner, M.D.

Garnering Capital
Make the Right Decisions.
Penetrate the Market.
Achieve Profitability.

ISBN 978-0-9748103-7-9

Business & Investing; Small Business & Entrepreneurship;
New Business Enterprises; Management & Leadership; Entrepreneurship;
Venture Capital; Business & Economics; Small Business; Biotech Startups.

Collaborative writing services: Judy Katz, ghostbooksters.com
Cover art direction: Wendy Glavin, ghostbooksters.com,
Cover & book design: Rebecca Saraceno, RebeccaInk
Copy editing and proofreading: Bonnie Egan

"At times our own light goes out and is rekindled by a spark from another person. Each of us has cause to think with deep gratitude of those who have lighted the flame within us."

— ALBERT SCHWEITZER

This book is dedicated, with great respect and admiration, to all the generous souls who have rekindled the flame of my sometimes disheartened spirit.

You know who you are!

Thank you, my friends and colleagues, for giving me your encouragement, wisdom — and at times even your financial support! — in the pursuit of my entrepreneurial and socially significant goals.

TABLE OF CONTENTS

ACKNOWLEDGEMENTS

NO ONE OPERATES in a vacuum, and I have been fortunate to work with some of the most brilliant, dynamic and encouraging individuals on this often times bumpy road. I especially want to single out the singular Lesa Mitchell, a key person at the Ewing Marion Kauffman Foundation, the globally-respected entrepreneurial foundation and incubator. Lesa has been and continues to be a treasured colleague and friend in the trajectory of my professional career.

This book has been a long time hatching, and editor extraordinaire Judy Katz has been my collaborator throughout. Thank you Judy for believing in my message and for your invaluable assistance in helping me get it out in the right way.

In addition to those who appear in the book, I would like to thank Amie Franklin for her analytical skill and for a decade of working shoulder to shoulder with me; Herman Chor for all the late nights and entrepreneurial flair; Ken Snoke for always being good natured; Peg Gilbert for being my "favorite aunt," and Jim & Gigi Kuo for showing how you can combine start-ups and family.

I also want to express my deep appreciation to Jim O'Brien for helpful comments and for telling my family that I am not crazy and Jayson Slotnik for reimbursement expertise, but more importantly for being a great friend. Thanks also to Trish Costello, Richard Bond and Heather Giles, Lowell Parsons, Ron Richards and Deborah Solomon for their always unconditional support when things get tough. Likewise my gratitude to

Michael Farber for his passionate intellectual property work, and to Dennis Brown for all his compassion and open-mindedness.

I also owe a deep debt of gratitude to Ashley Benjamin, David Tousley, Paul and Sue MacLeman, Andrew Lord, H.E. Mom Luong Rajadarasri, Jayankura and Paul Stinson for seeing the glass as half full; to Eric Adams for his jokes, which often gave me that much-needed laugh, and Mark Betteridge for his support of Jeff Bacha and me. An epic thank you to Peter Crisell for always lending his home in London as part of the "Bath Road Association;" to Kasia Pirog for being the coolest pathologist known to mankind, and the talented Peter Schlosshauer for tolerating us mere mortals. Thanks likewise to Jack Wands, Hubert Blum, Suzanne de la Monte, Fritz v. Weizsacker and Margherita Melegari, all of whom taught me a lot about science and even more about life.

I also want to express my heartfelt appreciation to these most generous colleagues and friends: Dwight Oxley, Tom Lee, Tom Heebink, Tom Kowalski, Kay Tieman, the Jeters, Ben McGraw, Bob Watkins, George Lasezkay, Seth Yakatan, Greg McKee, Jim Kemp, Fred Volinsky, Barry Selick, Tom Jurgensen, Benson Fong, Rhoda Payne, Mrs. Eulitt, Michael Goldberg, Tuya, Jessie Kim, Liz Carrington, Angus Tilney, Elizabeth Hill, Martin Berger, Lynne McElhinney, Alex Gerzenshtein, Jeff Jonas and Emmitt Jolly, Jim Tuffield, Jim Ryan and Jessica Bella Mura, Joe Merlino, Geoff Sargent, Nick Hanania, Hector, Jeff Proctor and Joel Teichman. And to John Warren: John, thank you for "getting" tech transfer.

How can I fully thank The Heckmans for being the coolest family I know, Lenian Shen for taking me all over China and being a friend my entire adult life, Mike Katovich for allowing me to practically major in his courses in college, Ken Lynn and Lindsay Rosenwald for giving me my first real job? I also want to acknowledge the deep contributions to my work and purpose made by Fred Mermelstein, Karl Ruggeberg, Steve Kanzer, Scott Beall, Tom Duley, Tom Dooley, Gary Holzsager, Chris and Dawn Heath and Russell Ellison.

And thank yous to Jay Lefkowitch, Karl Perzin, Diane Hamele-Bena, Peter Fisher, Tom Wright, Eugene Marc Antonio and K. O'Toole for being outstanding professors of pathology, each in his or her own distinct way.

I want to sincerely thank Terry Enfield for sorting out my finances; Lowell Mandelblatt, Peter Molloy, Daniel Green for our periodic dinners; Don Santel for our tennis matches, which were more meetings and therapy sessions, and Ashmeet Sidana for being right about everything. How can I ever adequately thank the too soon departed Bud Payne, Vaughn Mulder and Jim Daly? And likewise Sir James Black for his priceless support of Richard Bond and Inverseon.

Most importantly, my love and appreciation to my incredible parents, James and Carol Garner, and to the lovely Sandy Zou for putting up with me on a daily basis.

"Many of life's failures are people who did not realize how close they were to success when they gave up."

— THOMAS EDISON

INTRODUCTION

A PERSONAL PERSPECTIVE ON TAKING YOUR BREAKTHROUGH IDEA, TECHNOLOGY OR PRODUCT TO MARKET

I **HAVE FOUNDED THREE COMPANIES** in the health care arena. All the technologies have worked and all have been financed — one publicly. Additionally, I have been an angel investor, vested in the development and growth of other companies I believed had important or even disruptive technologies or products to bring to market, and a better than fifty percent chance of success. I was out to "do well while doing good."

Initially however, in addition to being idealistic and ambitious I was also naïve. I thought much needed advances made in the laboratory would normally be brought into the real world to help humanity. I thought companies that set and reached key milestones would typically be funded. What I discovered was how different — and difficult — these objectives were in the real world. That is my reason for writing this book. Think of it as a little GPS: Hopefully I can point out some of the inevitable obstacles and provide you some useful alternate routes to get to where you need to go.

My hope is that my experience and examples will make the process of creating, discovering, building, funding or promoting the Next Big Thing the world is waiting for so much easier and makes you so rich that you can easily meet Warren Buffett's philanthropic challenge and donate a few million dollars to the Gates Foundation.

Overly optimistic perhaps, but as coach Vince Lombardi put it: "I firmly believe that any man's finest hour, the greatest fulfillment of all that he holds dear, is the moment when he has worked his heart out in a good cause and lies exhausted on the field of battle — victorious."

Perhaps even more relevant to the subject of this book is what Sumner Redstone tells us: "Success is not built on success. It's built on failure. It's built on frustration. Sometimes it's built on catastrophe."

Think of innovation as the love child of imagination and practical necessity. A new drug, a new technology, an improved way of doing something that makes it faster, easier, more accessible — these are all the result of fertile minds that seek to make the world a better place in one way or another. The desire to achieve distinction is a great motivator and there is nothing wrong with enjoying a measure of fame and fortune and leaving a legacy along the way. Innovators are those restless souls among us who have no other choice but to follow their passion, driven to give birth to something new in service to mankind.

But for artists and all "creators" the world has changed, and the rules of the game have shifted. No kings or queens or Medicis are around to support the scientist, the inventor, the mathematician and the dreamer. Now it is the angel investors, venture capitalists, the hedge funds and investment banks that must be satisfied. Most require a business plan, of course. They need to believe that you and your team envision and can carry out a clear path to success and eventual profitability, hopefully sooner rather than later. Sometimes it works beautifully for the good of all concerned. Sometimes the system breaks down, and your potential Next Big Thing shrivels and dies for lack of the critical funding that can take it to the necessary next stage.

To be honest, it is not the system that breaks down, because it is scalable — if entrepreneurs truly understand what it is like for early stage investors, and vice versa. Both will need to embrace, to some extent at least, the inevitable ambiguity, which creates the potential to shift a paradigm and make 10 times or 100 times on an investment. In my experience, the derailing factor, most often, is the inability of both the innovator and the investor to find and understand each other in the right way at the right time. It's almost like a romance — two entities seeking union pass each other in the dark, unaware of what might have been, if only they could have connected.

This, then, is what *Garnering Capital* is intended to be, a place where the roads converge. In other words, to show innovators how they can find financial support, and to also show those willing to support innovators how to find and intelligently evaluate them so that both parties can work together to make this planet we share a far better — not to mention far healthier — world for every one of us.

As I sought to create new ventures with innovative technologies, it soon became clear that the challenges of assembling the necessary components, especially the intellectual property and capital, were becoming increasingly difficult, for a variety of reasons. In an environment of flat federal funding for many areas of investigation, scientists must become more entrepreneurial. The "star system" is also becoming a bigger factor, with the winners taking most of the largest grants and awards. At the same time, we hear from the renowned Kauffman Foundation and others how important these interfaces of human endeavor are to our nation, to help keep us competitive on the world stage and a leader in innovation. Sometimes it seems, as heard in conversations between inventors, entrepreneurs and investors, that the parties involved are not speaking the same language. At the risk of sounding like I've been living in California for too long, we certainly need to understand one another's motivations better, and need to communicate more effectively.

Dealing with university technology transfer offices, for example, can be an exercise in frustration for entrepreneurs. Are technology transfer people motivated to maximize the number of deals they do? Are they incentivized to get paperwork done at the pace of private enterprise? On both counts, I think not. So, who is at fault? Is it the faculty? The heads of research? But those are the same key people who invent the innovations we need, so why would they put obstacles in their own paths?

And, from the entrepreneur's perspective, why is it that we view all university technologies as having a negative net present value (NPV)? In other words, why do the business people calculate current worth of a product discounted back from market assumptions? But they do, continually, and this is a seeming contradiction when we go to license a technology. These university-born technologies suddenly become quite valuable! Interestingly, in my experience, this phenomenon occurs even when a given technology has been sitting on a shelf for years. I would argue assignment (a transfer of ownership) is a more constructive form of moving innovations to market.

Speaking from my experience, the entrepreneur must be prepared to negotiate for the rights to a given technology for at least one to two years. It therefore makes sense to identify multiple technologies and negotiate on a number of fronts — "hedging your bets" so to speak. Of course there is no guarantee that *any* of the deals will close on reasonable terms. But inventors are by nature emotionally tied to their inventions, as parents to offspring. It can be no surprise that one's life work has the ability to stir deep emotion. This is why the process of bringing their inventions to market often breaks down for them.

Having lived through many of these breakdowns, I know what it takes to be knocked down in the ring and get up, bruised and bloodied, to fight another round. I wrote this tome for other roadshow warriors and their suitors. This is not a how-to book but rather a candid overview of my personal experience, laced with suggestions from a few key experts on how to proceed. All we want to do is give you insights from the frontlines, "dirty laundry" and all, on how inventors can partner with entrepreneurs, and vice versa, to streamline the process of bringing a new drug, technology or other innovative product or service to market in the best possible way.

I believe inventors and business people can successfully partner and take their inventions or products out into the world in a practical, effective way. It always begins with negotiations, and the first negotiation will, of course, be with the university. The next negotiation for inventor/entrepreneur will be with potential investors. These will eventually be professional investors (institutional investors, hedge funds and investment banks) but more likely at this early point you will be negotiating mainly with angel investors and venture capitalists.

How do I know all this? Why am I qualified to share my knowledge with you? Have you seen my battle scars?

Please, read on...

GARNERING CAPITAL

"He who has a why to live can bear almost any how."

— FRIEDRICH NIETZSCHE

1

THE SOUL PURPOSES OF THE INNOVATIVE ENTREPRENEUR

LIFE ISN'T EASY for entrepreneurs — those who have the drive and determination to build and run a business, whether specifically in the medical, pharmaceutical or overall health care arena or in some other industry. It is especially challenging to learn how to persevere and keep perspective (as well as sanity and a sense of humor) when the funds needed to keep their ventures on track and growing are difficult to come by.

Within that group of people with entrepreneurial souls is another kind of business innovator: the doctor or researcher turned entrepreneurial inventor. These are men and women who feel the call to help treat and, hopefully, even perhaps help find a cure for one or another of the terrible diseases or conditions that continue to plague mankind. Scientists, inventors, entrepreneurs, founders and CEOs: all are strivers within the biotech, pharmaceutical, medical device or similar arena in the overall health care industry. I am one of these people, and I can tell you that our lot is not always a happy one. Most of us are finding the gentle (funding) waves of yesteryear to be elusive these days, with no warnings of the dangerous underwater rock formations ahead as our little ships fight their ways forward in the roiling waves. With money and time in short supply, competition is fierce, and rejection lurks around every corner. Nevertheless, despite the odds stacked against us, we keep moving onward — perhaps foolhardily sometimes — because we must.

In our darkest hours, we may look to another entrepreneur/inventor, who believed that there was no such thing as failure, only 9,999 ways to not build a light bulb. In his time, many labeled Thomas Edison foolishly persistent. Like him, we will endure anything to arrive at that milestone: the 10,000th try that takes. In the meantime, what we — you and I — all too often have to endure can boggle the mind and leave us gasping for breath.

However, there in fact is a whole economy of people wanting to help you. Play your cards right, and many will. But if you are not careful, some may end up picking your pocket. It could be those working at the local incubator, or the gentleman who runs the accounting firm you use. Probably the biggest risk of getting an unexpected bill would be from an attorney. It is essential to get all of these relationships right. It is also important to not be penny wise and pound foolish while yes, certainly being efficient and making the best tradeoffs. Essentially the challenge is to survive while not throwing too much overboard.

A lot of raising angel capital is about perceptions, not unlike politics. Angel groups can be excellent sources of money, but the bigger they are, the more they operate like VCs, just without the same deep pockets.

So much of being an entrepreneur cannot be anticipated. One has to keep one's bearings. The human relationships and judgments we make about our investors and colleagues can be the difference between success and failure, much more than the contracts.

Jeff Bezos' family famously signed their $300K retirement fund over to him as he was founding Amazon. This is where the initial capital comes from for many of us. Whether we are trying to cure cancer or open a dental practice or insurance agency, you go to family and friends first. In my case that was not an option, because there was no big retirement fund to tap, but if it's an option for you, more power to you.

One popular definition of entrepreneurship is that it is "the process of creating or seizing an opportunity and pursuing it regardless of the resources currently controlled." (Jeffry Timmons) Translation: You have to be resourceful above all else. Besides going the friends and family route, maxing out your credit cards, taking a second mortgage on your home and the like, it might also mean doing your elevator speech in actual elevators or on the street. Or it might mean going public without an investment bank, as I will discuss later on. These are the types of things you have to be prepared to do, and they are mild compared to some of the situations I have found myself in over the years, as I too, perhaps like you, have attempted to push forward my "brilliant" ideas and projects.

In general, the biggest challenge is not that someone is going to steal your idea, but that you are going to have to differentiate your new business from all others in your arena, and then find and engage the right people to join your team and inspire others to fund you. You must make what you are up to not only relevant but critically imperative to the needs of your colleagues, investors and, ultimately, to patients or customers.

At the end of the day, we do the things we do for reasons that are intrinsic rather than extrinsic. Understanding those motivations in ourselves and others is central to successful outcomes for the innovator/entrepreneur and those who invest with us. As long as the products we are developing have the potential to meaningfully impact hundreds of thousands or even millions of lives, people like you and I will continue to practice our trade.

What is it in my background, you might wonder, that qualifies me to even try to untangle the hellishly complex Gordian Knot that holds inventors, entrepreneurs, venture capitalists, intellectual property lawyers and practicing physicians together? The short answer is that I have worn almost all of those hats, however ill-fitting some of them may have been, in various development projects in which I have participated throughout my career. The longer answer is a bit more complicated.

Looking back, as a medical student I was already entrepreneurial as I transferred medical schools, created my own research year, including time in Switzerland, and was generally a pain to my deans. I have always been interested in the various technologies that physicians employ and how that best translates to the clinical experience. The interface between science and medicine is pathology, and studying that I began to see how things progressed from the laboratory bench into the patient's milieu. This has traditionally been a poorly understood aspect of medical care. I am not a trained scientist and was not even a science major in my undergraduate years, but I had the good fortune to do my training during an era when molecular biology was changing the way we understood human physiology and disease. Doctors were encouraged to ask out-of-the-box questions and pursue treatment regimens undreamt of by colleagues who went before. The modern analogy might be with the Internet, which in a few short years managed to grant access to the cyber-equivalent of the Library of Congress to anyone with a modem. Molecular biology has been called "science without a license" by Ph.Ds, in particular when practiced by MDs!

One of the great shocks that I got when I first began practicing medicine was how tremendous the inefficiencies could sometimes be. Just walking around a medical center can be frustrating. In my case, it was Columbia Presbyterian Medical Center in New York. Getting from one part of the complex to another might require going on three elevator rides, through three electronic locks, and over an elevated bridge just to get one small thing done, then going back and retracing your steps. When I was on the elevated bridge, I could see Manhattan in the distance. I too was in Manhattan, but at its extreme upper end, so I sometimes felt like I was spending most of my time in this tube-bridge going back and forth, thanks (or actually no thanks) to some arbitrary decision an architect made before I was born.

I wanted to be involved in endeavors that created revenue in an efficient and effective manner, so I began to think about the strengths and weaknesses of the entire medical system. With this maze I just described being a metaphor for many things that were not well thought out and therefore inefficient and wasteful, I decided to practice what I call innovation medicine (@InnovationMD on Twitter). In other words, to become an entrepreneur. I guess another definition of entrepreneurship is doing business without a license!

Much medical innovation is pharmaceutical in nature. After my medical training I spent time in both large and small pharmaceutical companies, learning how they did things, and what shaped their research priorities. Not surprisingly, the large companies were focused on developing those drugs that had the maximum potential for revenue generation. Sometimes this meant that companies, both large and small, would develop drugs that improve a patient's appearance or accomplish some other relatively trivial feat before they would develop drugs that treated a rare or chronic disease, based purely on economic considerations. The smaller companies had more of a sense of urgency since, generally speaking, at least a third of these small companies do not have enough cash to operate for more than a year and, as a result, frequently lack the resources needed to bring their new products to market. Their survival depends on their ability to acquire investment partners and secure the necessary resources. What I observed was that the best small companies treasured innovation more than large ones did, which made them powerfully attractive under the right circumstances.

Arguably, MDs are not welcome in the pharmaceutical industry. If they are it is generally required of them to have been trained as an internist, which I was not. So I looked for other avenues where I could more easily contribute. I had learned a critical lesson: that innovation takes time, frequently unpredictable amounts of time. Often one person who is tenacious can make the difference in whether or not an innovation is eventually adopted. For someone like myself, who saw product development as an extension of medical practice, or a kind of meta-practice, I needed to commit to doing this over the long haul. This would become my life's work, and success would require more than great medical ideas. It would also require a thorough understanding of how products gain entry to their proper position in the marketplace.

To continue my education in innovation medicine, I took a job on Wall Street, working with a company that had (and still has) a long history of taking on innovative ideas and making them realities. They do this by underwriting their development and providing them with a vastly improved corporate structure. While some people term the stock market and venture capital formation as "legalized gambling," I take a very different, more positive view, but of course you need to pick your spots carefully. Breakthrough inventions very rarely occur anymore in the isolated garage or dank basement of the sole tinkerer. Instead, they are accomplished by teams of scientists using expensive equipment. These inventions or other types of breakthroughs must undergo severe regulatory scrutiny, especially if they involve medicine and patient health. Development costs are enormous, and the risks are great. Spreading the risk over many investors and many products is the most prudent tack to take.

With these experiences, I am often asked why I did not go into academics, where scientific research is a major part of a university's mission.

Part of the reason is the increasing cost of developing new drugs and procedures. If a university researcher comes up with a new solution, he or she will at some point probably end up seeking corporate investment, especially since university endowments are no more equipped for modern product development than are basement laboratories. Also, there are limits to what research can be done in universities, especially publicly funded ones. At a time when there is no moral consensus on such hot-button topics as stem cell research, animal testing protocols, cloning, and even the proper relationship of the non-profit university to the for-profit corporation, the comparative shelter and security of a university appointment is not sufficient to compensate for these evolving uncertainties and their often frustratingly slow pace of progress.

The satisfying part of this work, for me, lies in determining what the greatest unmet medical needs are and then developing approaches to meeting these needs. I study the literature like every other physician, but I have found that evaluating new ideas and approaches is very much a human contact sport. It is easier to cut through the formalities in the doctors' lounge through direct conversation than try to read between the lines in the literature.

I set out to be involved in projects and companies that I estimated should take three years or less to develop, and for which an approval could be obtained for approximately ten to fifteen million dollars. These are typically not new chemical entities (brand new drugs), but adjustments. For example, this includes changing the route of administration for a drug, or changing the way a drug is dosed or delivered, or even filing new regulatory documents and bringing it into a part of the world where it has not been commercialized. Testing protocols and regulatory hurdles are smaller when this approach is adopted; and, not insignificantly, the internal rates of return for our investors tend to be higher, with a lower ante required.

All well and good you may say, but how *does* that breakthrough idea get out from behind the closed doors of a respected university's research laboratory and into the real world? Turn the page, and read on.....

GARNER'S RULES FOR THE ROAD

- The challenge is to survive while not throwing too much overboard.
- The human relationships and judgments we make about our investors and colleagues can spell the difference between success and failure.
- You must make what you are up to not only relevant but critically imperative to the needs of your colleagues, investors and, ultimately, to customers.
- Understanding our motivations and those of others is central to successful outcomes for the innovator/entrepreneur and those who invest with us.
- The best small companies seem to treasure innovation more than large ones do.
- Often one person who is tenacious can make the difference in whether an innovation is eventually adopted.
- Work with many projects: spreading risk over many investors and many products is the most prudent tack to take.
- University endowments are no more equipped for modern product development than are basement laboratories.
- Above all else, you have to be resourceful.

"If you have an apple and I have an apple and we exchange these apples then you and I will still each have one apple. But if you have an idea and I have an idea and we exchange these ideas, then each of us will have two ideas."

— GEORGE BERNARD SHAW

2

THE OFTEN DIFFICULT JOURNEY FROM UNIVERSITY LAB TO REAL-WORLD APPLICATION

FOR THIS TOPIC I have enlisted the help of Lesa Mitchell, Vice President of Innovation at the Ewing Marion Kauffman Foundation, where she shares her insights and extensive frontline experience at one of the country's most innovative and exciting foundations and innovation incubators. She will also tell you, in her own words, how the foundation officer connects entrepreneurial partners with inventors, researchers and scientists working within universities.

The Kauffman Foundation is perhaps the greatest legacy of Ewing Marion Kauffman, founder of Marion Labs. Mr. Kauffman was and still is without question the biggest hero in Kansas City, which is my hometown. I remember my father telling me his story at a Kansas City Royals baseball game (Mr. K owned the team). Mr. Kauffman was a sales representative for a pharmaceutical company and evidently a great one — so good in fact that they repeatedly cut his commission rates. He began Marion Labs in his own home, crushing oyster shells to make a calcium supplement. He called the firm by his middle name, Marion, so no one would know his company was a one-person operation. From that start, he grew Marion Labs to over $1 billion in sales. He took good care of his employees, who shared in the wealth. In 1993, Kauffman left some $1 billion to his foundation for their important work, which Lesa will describe. In her important role, she is at the heart of the Kauffman Foundation and an effective connector for entrepreneurs around the globe.

I was introduced to Lesa by Trish Costello, who ran the Kauffman Fellow's Program, initially conceived to expand diversity in the venture capital industry for its first ten years. Lesa had asked me to put together some war stories from tech transfer negotiations in which I was involved. A year or two later, I was privileged to participate in one small part of Kauffman's work: improving technology commercialization. Lesa sent me, along with a former president of the Association of University Technology Managers (AUTM) and one of her Kauffman colleagues, to seven campuses to interview professors, as well as senior university administration and technology transfer officers.

All the institutions we visited had brilliant faculty, but were located outside of the Northeast and California. They also generally did not have medical schools and had annual research budgets of less than $300 million, compared to the billion-dollar annual budgets of some elite universities.

The institutions with all of these characteristics tend to see a further dividend to collaborating with "outsiders" in a boost in funding of about 3% that occurs annually in donations and further sponsored research. Additionally, the capital backing they receive has many other collateral benefits, including an enhanced reputation and better students and faculty, which in turn beget more of the same.

What the Kauffman Foundation learned over time is that while academics could be a lot more collaborative with business, they are essentially internally focused, with professors, administration and technology transfer administrators understanding one another better than they understand the world of business that lies outside the university walls. They also don't necessarily want to do more business because they value it less than other rewards.

No one who knows Lesa is quite sure how she keeps up her pace year in and year out, but I am glad she does, since her efforts, and those of her colleagues at the Kauffman Foundation, are important not just to us entrepreneurs, but to U.S. competitiveness.

The following much appreciated background information and important strategic advice is in Lesa's words...

Thanks, Bill, for this opportunity to "speak" to your readers. Let me tell you about the Ewing Marion Kauffman Foundation and why this may be important to your readers. As the world's largest foundation devoted to entrepreneurship and the only U.S. foundation to focus on entrepreneurs, the Ewing Marion Kauffman Foundation does many things. It supports many entrepreneurship research centers at universities, including MIT, New York University, University of California at Berkeley, University of Illinois, University of Kansas, University of North Carolina at Chapel Hill, and Washington University. It helps develop curriculum materials to teach entrepreneurship to college and high school students. Its Urban Entrepreneur Partnership (UEP) program helps mentor small fledgling businesses in the devastated Hurricane Katrina region and elsewhere.

The way the Kauffman Foundation aims to make the biggest difference in advancing innovation is by its work to improve the outcomes of university research, and its efforts to help translate discoveries made at universities to practical use. In other words, Kauffman is helping universities become more entrepreneurial, more nurturing, and more welcoming to the kinds of new ideas needed for an entrepreneurial economy. We believe universities, industry and government need to collaborate more to spark a rich cross-pollination of ideas, recognize their interdependence, and give up petty snobberies and defensiveness about their own bailiwicks. By so doing they will create what my boss, Kauffman's chief executive Carl J. Schramm, calls an "ecosystem of innovation."

Necessity may be the mother of invention, as the old cliché goes, but free and open collaboration is the promoter of invention, Kauffman believes, and so has taken practical steps to foster it. Like many great entrepreneurial teams, there is a kind of "outside" and "inside" pairing. Carl realized this great opportunity and challenge, and charged me with implementing his vision. For my part, this successful collaboration is a task I work on tirelessly.

Our country's investment in research and knowledge must replace the manufacturing plants that served as the engines of economic growth after World War II, and our university researchers must fill that gap. Thus, it's of paramount importance to foster a fertile environment where ideas are generated and put to the best possible use.

A study reported in 2007 by Marks and Clerk, a British law firm, found that during the years 2002-2006 among the world's top 20 patent filing entities for patent production, university academics beat out corporations by 51%. In biotechnology, the most influential patents, as measured by frequency in citations, are all held by U.S. universities, with MIT and Harvard tied at the top.

THE PLUSES OF UNIVERSITY-INDUSTRY COLLABORATIONS

It's illuminating to note the history of successful university-industry collaborations and see why fostering this is so important. One of the most fruitful is Genentech Inc., now part of Roche. *Wired* magazine cites it as an organization capable of "sustained innovation," developing breakthrough products and creating new business models. Co-founded in 1976 by a University of California at San Francisco professor of biochemistry and biophysics, Dr. Herbert Boyer, and venture capitalist Robert Swanson, Genentech is a maker and marketer of the anti-cancer drug Avastin® for brain, colon and lung cancer, Herceptin® for breast cancer, and Lucentis® for age-related macular degeneration, which is the main cause of blindness.

Wired also cited Genentech's "X factor" — a hunger for new ideas and impatience to give them practical applications. Genentech's former CEO, Arthur Levinson, once said, "If you want an innovative environment, hire innovative people, listen to them tell you what they want, and do it."

But this brilliant university-industry collaboration wouldn't have happened unless Swanson, the VC, had not called Dr. Boyer, the director of his university's graduate genetics program, and set up a meeting to discuss developing products from recombinant DNA. At the time the industry didn't really recognize the commercial potential of biology-based technologies. But Swanson did; he held a bachelor's degree in chemistry from MIT as well as a graduate degree from its Sloan School of Business. The visionary former partner of the Silicon Valley venture capital firm Kleiner Perkins became Genentech's CEO until 1990, then its chairman of the board. This story is well-known in entrepreneurial circles, but always worth repeating.

Some other stellar examples of university-industry collaboration: Emory University chemistry professor Dennis Liotta, who co-founded two companies to bring his drug discoveries to market — Pharmasset and Triangle (both today part of Gilead) and engineering professor Alberto Sangiovanni-Vincentelli of the University of California at Berkeley, co-founder of two design technology companies. The compound used in drug cocktails for HIV patients, 3TC, was co-developed by Professor Liotta with an academic colleague. Dr. Liotta firmly believed that a smaller, focused firm is often better at dealing with a new drug discovery than a pharmaceutical giant, who may ignore the discovery. Professor Liotta was also involved in other start-ups. Then there's his non-profit, which aims to harness scientific talent in Africa and develop better drugs to combat the "big three" diseases that ravage that continent: AIDS, malaria and tuberculosis.

Professor Sangiovanni-Vincentelli came to Berkeley, a center for research in computer-aided microchip design, in 1976, and in 1982 ended up co-founding, with Berkeley's dean of engineering Richard Newton, the start-up SDA Systems, Inc., which later became Cadence Design. The pair succeeded in getting $4 million in seed capital from potential customers in industry, and they co-founded Synopsys five years later.

Today, both Cadence and Synopsys are billion-dollar providers of electronic design automation software, used to design microchips, and have thousands of employees. It's no surprise that Professor Sangiovanni-Vincentelli believes that far more university research should be shared openly instead of patented and licensed, and that freely-circulating ideas can change the world. His research was achieved open-domain, where his software tools could be downloaded free to anyone who wanted them, and he consulted with large microchip-makers. Berkeley received no licensing fees from any of his activities, but the university benefited from donations and the industry-sponsored research that followed.

Entrepreneurs in the life sciences owe a great debt to our counterparts in high technology. The can-do culture is infectious in the Bay Area and has made it easier to found life science and other types of businesses and to have the flexibility they need to succeed. After all, entrepreneurs should enjoy the journey. We hope this instructs our colleagues in technology transfer as well.

THE INDIVIDUAL RESEARCHER VS. THE UNIVERSITY

When Kauffman began to study how to improve the outcomes of university research, it assumed patenting and licensing was the most important model — that university researchers invent or discover an innovation, file for a patent, and then the patent is licensed, either to an existing firm or a start-up formed specifically to capitalize on it. Instead, what Kauffman discovered is that patenting and licensing isn't the only model, or even the best model, to transfer a discovery from the university to the marketplace — it's just one of many.

Too often, universities focus "inordinately" on patenting and licensing at the expense of what really sparks innovation. Kauffman isn't alone in noticing the flaws of the patent-and-license model; the Federal Trade Commission and National Academy of Sciences are among many others calling for reform of our patent system, as it no longer promotes innovation as well as it should.

In fact, studies have shown that an individual academic researcher often is more adept in identifying opportunities for practical application of his or her research than a university's technology transfer office. University technology transfer offices that handle the negotiations are frequently overburdened and understaffed, which can delay licensing new technology — while in many industries time is of the essence. When technology transfer offices stubbornly hold out for high fees, there are even more delays.

Research faculty themselves are the key agents of knowledge transfer. One study by UCLA researchers Lynne Zucker and Michael Darby, published in a National Bureau of Economic Research working paper and supported by the Kauffman Foundation, highlights the fact that "star" university faculty drive the formation of high-tech firms, not their inventions as isolated entities. In fact, high rates of patenting and licensing at a university were not always linked to regions that had high levels of innovative commercial activity, but to universities with high numbers of "star" faculty, that are defined as those publishing research articles cited often by others. Indeed, the universities with "stars" on faculty were correlated with regions that showed high levels of commercial innovation — for example, the Boston/Cambridge area and Silicon Valley. The universities in other countries also adhered to this pattern, UCLA researchers found.

Universities also send mixed messages to faculty. How? By granting tenure on the basis of publishing papers and winning grants, and disparaging corporate consulting as sidetracking an academic from his or her true work. This implies that moving science to market is not that important. The exception, however, is if the academic has invented something of obvious great commercial value — in which case the technology transfer office will jump on it and try to extract from it as much revenue as possible. Still, many promising technologies languish in university laboratories, Kauffman studies found. This is because their usefulness is not that obvious, because universities overemphasize "big hit" potential or patentable possibilities, or because they are useful only if combined with other technologies that researchers may not know about.

Senior faculty members have the power to incentivize technology transfer officers. We were advising a tech transfer office once, working in their offices three or four days a month. One officer was often seen leaving before four o'clock p.m. Later we noticed the same officer had begun to stay until well after nine o'clock. What was happening? As we later learned, a faculty member had given him a modest equity position in a raw start-up; thus incentivized, he was enthusiastically doing additional research after hours on potential markets for this company.

BUILDING RELATIONSHIPS WITH INDUSTRY

Kauffman advises university faculty about how critically important it is for them to have frequent contacts with industry. This can be through consulting with companies, serving on advisory boards, doing research sponsored by industry, etc. There are multiple benefits for faculty to transmit their knowledge to industry directly. Their thinking becomes more attuned to practical applications. They build mutually supportive social networks in the marketplace. They can spark innovation in the next generation of students and younger researchers by mentoring them. They also become more apt to patent and license and they become better at it.

The chilling effect of the overemphasis by U.S. universities on earning revenue via licensing ends up driving up costs. Even worse, their over-protective attitude toward intellectual property generated by university researchers has resulted in more industry-sponsored university research taking place outside the U.S., especially in India and China. In other countries there is often more access to top university researchers and greater ease of collaboration with these researchers. Companies that sponsor university research must help finance research, and then pay again to license results, because, under the dictates of the Bayh-Dole Act, universities own the intellectual property for innovations resulting from federally funded research.

THE SOLUTIONS: MAINSTREAMING INNOVATION

One practical step the foundation took to advance innovations at universities into the mainstream was creating the iBridge Network (www.ibridgenetwork.org). This free Website allows universities to post information about their discoveries and research methods — for potential sale or free use — and network among themselves. Industry can also learn about these innovations, do one-stop-shopping to find them, and buy them through online licensing and eCommerce tools. So can entrepreneurs, who may find innovations to spur new ventures. You can search for innovations by field — from life and physical sciences to various categories of information technology; and from drug discoveries, software, and diagnostics to bioinformatics by university, keyword or "what's hot" (such as cancer, DNA, gene therapy).

This is the first pilot program of the Kauffman Innovation Network Inc., established in 2005, which piloted this program with several major universities. The universities are disseminating news about iBridge by making presentations to academic departments and individual researchers and by attending conferences. Hundreds of research projects have been posted, and success stories resulting from this free and easy exchange of ideas are growing. One University of Chicago researcher sold a copy of her software that analyzes changes in hormone levels to Harvard Medical School two days after posting it.

Another step Kauffman is taking is to help universities encourage technology transfer offices to increase the number of licenses for innovations — the way some elite successful research universities already do — instead of maintaining a myopic focus on maximizing license income. This outreach asks universities to relinquish the assumption that licensing revenue is the only, or main, form of "payback" for innovation, and embrace more of a macro view of its rewards. University innovations can spur generous donations from grateful companies and alumni, increase industry-sponsored research in the U.S., and build an image of the university as an exciting place where faculty can do groundbreaking research. This in turn lures and keeps faculty "stars," which draws more research grants and donations and likewise draws the most talented students, in a most beneficent domino effect.

Thank you, Lesa. Clearly success begets more success, and innovation begets more innovation, in a self-reinforcing loop. The goal, as Lesa often says, is "innovation flowing out of the university through multiple pathways, with the rewards cycling back through many paths."

Clearly bringing industry and academia together can yield significant results, even if the project you begin with is a modest one. I also want to make the point that this collaboration can be initiated the other way around, coming from the opposite direction so to speak, when industry goes into the laboratory. My experience in this realm began when I moved to Vancouver in 2004 and spent a few years there. During that time, I developed a valuable network, not just in British Columbia but throughout Canada.

Years later, I was able to leverage those connections in founding DelMar Pharmaceuticals, Inc. with two business partners. Our lead program was initially brain cancer, specifically the treatment of Glioblastoma (GBM). With DelMar Pharmaceuticals, we did something different in our approach to intellectual property. It took extra creativity on the part of one of my co-founders, but over time he accessed information on drugs in the public domain, specifically in the field of oncology, and modernized it in terms of clinical use and manufacturing processes. This new use of an older and now updated technology became our own intellectual property.

We then brought our technology to a university professor and asked her to use it in her laboratory, through research we would sponsor or find sponsors for. The good parts of industry-academic partnership work still happen. New insights, excellent abstracts and publications are generated but we are not encumbered by a license from the university tied to their technology that we have to live with for our entire corporate life. Instead of protracted negotiations with a university, we have focused our energies on valuable collaborations with large industrial partners in Asia. These entities do not have operations in North America and view us as a good way to begin to work more with Westerners.

One of the DelMar co-founders, Dennis Brown, Ph.D, who was a former client of my company, EGB, had previously founded a company with the same business model — modernization of an older cancer drug studied extensively in the U.S. but only commercialized, distributed and sold in China. That company was acquired in 2011 for approximately $350 million, including EU rights. Several other companies with this exact business model have been acquired for $200 to $500 million.

Our other co-founder, Jeff Bacha, is on the ground in Vancouver, where he has spent over a decade building relationships in the life sciences start-up community and the Canadian public markets. Jeff was able to secure an early grant for DelMar that allowed us to study the mechanism of our drug at the University of British Columbia. By doing this, we stumbled upon very important data, which we believe explains why our drug has the potential to work well for cancer patients while current front-line therapy fails in 60% of these same types of patients. DelMar has since opened an IND and initiated a phase I/IIa clinical trial in brain tumors. The first round of investment is structured to lead to a public transaction within the next year or so.

This is another approach, and another way to once again bring industry and academia together productively, for the greater good of all concerned.

LESA MITCHELL'S POINTS TO REMEMBER

- Innovation works best when it can travel many paths from one sector to another.
- World class research can exist not only inside the largest/most prestigious institutions but also outside, in much smaller institutions.
- Collaboration with industry has been shown to improve both commercial application and academic endeavor (i.e. garnering better grant scores).
- By maximizing outside collaboration, universities benefit financially in multiple ways.
- There are many ways to get technologies out of universities.
- The core values of individuals are an essential component for success, be they tech transfer officers, inventors or their far-sighted business partners and investors.

"Don't worry about people stealing your ideas. If your ideas are any good,you'll have to ram them down people's throats."

— HOWARD AIKEN (1900 – 1973)
PIONEER IN COMPUTING

3

SUCCESSFULLY PROTECTING YOUR IP AND TELLING YOUR STORY WELL

IN THIS CHAPTER I bring you insights from another expert: a highly effective Silicon Valley venture capitalist. Since Silicon Valley culture can teach a lot to those of us in the life sciences, I thought it would be helpful to go right to "the horse's mouth" and solicit this active, high profile VC's perspective on the two basic ways you can position yourself for success. One is by protecting your product or idea and the second, by attracting investors.

Although we always need to keep our focus on whatever technology we are in the midst of developing, it is likewise important to keep in mind just how competitive it is to garner attention — not to mention cash and credit — for an early-stage company. Ashmeet Sidana, General Partner, Foundation Capital, reminds us of these points as he offers up some essential guidance.

The following was written by Ashmeet:

Thanks, Bill, for letting me expound on my favorite subject. A venture capitalist's perennial challenge is to identify, invest money in and hopefully profit from the "next big thing." As a Silicon Valley VC, as well as a former entrepreneur in the ultra-competitive technology market, I have been responsible for some ideas of my own that turned out to be quite valuable, so I think I can help explain to your readers how to protect their great idea, product or technology.

BESIDES THE USUAL SUSPECTS...

Some ways to protect your intellectual property are obvious: patents, trademarks and copyrights. Others are less obvious but far more wide-ranging and oftentimes more effective. These include shaping your business model and working to gain brand recognition; in other words, creating a point of difference so that your product is first in the mind of the customer. If and when appropriate, you will also want to build a relationship with a company that has the ability to bring your idea to market. Of course, you will need to cement that understanding in a contractual agreement in order to keep competitors out — and trade secrets and "networking effects" in. All the things I discuss are ways that can, separately and together, work to safeguard your great idea or product, while strengthening its position in the market.

TOO MUCH EMPHASIS PLACED ON PATENTS AND TECHNOLOGY

A patent can be a disadvantage if it means that you put too much focus on a product or idea in general, and not enough on the customer who will use it. Before we talk about the narrower, legal ways to protect your product or idea — which as we said before includes patents, trademarks and copyrights — let's look at some real life examples that I believe you will find instructive.

YOUR BUSINESS MODEL: MARCH TO A DIFFERENT DRUMMER

If you're a car rental company, an airport is the place to be. As that old real estate mantra goes, it's all about "location, location, location." No question the airport assures an unlimited supply of customers in desperate need of a rental car. But after Hertz and Avis lock up the choice spots at airports, what's another car rental firm to do? Let's say that's you: You're blocked from a lucrative market, and have no legal way at your disposal to restrict these major competitors, who had such foresight. Wait: Enter Enterprise, an apt name for an enterprising company that simply found different markets where customers also needed to rent cars, for example, auto body shops. After all, when you leave your vehicle for repair, you are going to need another to drive away in.

In fact, by grabbing expensive airport space, Hertz and Avis locked themselves out of more moderately priced space for their car rental offices. The moral of this story? Yes, if you're Number Two, as Avis states in its ads, you certainly need to try harder. But if you're Number Three or Four or Ten, you need to think smarter. Sometimes surprising opportunities arise when the obvious routes are spoken for. The business model of Rent-a-Wreck, another competitor, wasn't about picking different locations but of offering the customer cheaper rental costs for non-premium cars — though frankly many are of better quality than the word "wreck" might suggest, and are part of several reasons why their customer base continues to build.

NETWORK EFFECTS: THE MORE THE MERRIER

When you're perceived as more valuable, you attract more customers than others do. That's the principle behind eBay, the New York Stock Exchange, Facebook, MySpace, YouTube and high-circulation magazines — as well as popular restaurants, popular bands, even popular women — any kind of marketplace or exchange. If you're in demand, you get to be in even greater demand because popularity begets more popularity. It's the buzz, the ripple effect; people go where the positive numbers are, where there's excitement, growth and lots of other people interested. This creates an exponential, multiplier phenomenon. That's why buyers go to eBay to find sellers, and sellers go there to meet buyers. It's why the premier stock exchange in the U.S. remains on top, why ads in magazines with lots of readers cost more than others. It's why YouTube was sold for such a whopping amount. It's why some restaurants are constantly booked and others suffer, and why men often chase after women who have a large "following" of eager suitors. You don't want to miss out; it's crowd psychology at work.

Fax machines are a good example. The first person in the world who bought a fax machine had a product that was totally useless. Who was he going to fax to? The second person who bought a fax had one person to send and receive faxes from — no real value. But the 100th person had dozens of people he/she could send material to. The network effect is very powerful and hard to overcome. It is never easy to be a newcomer; but this is not a cause for despair, because there are many ways to break in. Look at NASDAQ; look at some of the other social networking sites, and so on.

BRAND RECOGNITION: STAND FOR SOMETHING PEOPLE WANT

Being first to market is a great idea. But there is something more powerful: being first in the mind of the customer — the one who reaches for Bayer when they want an aspirin, who thinks of Kleenex when they need a tissue, turns Xerox into a synonym for copying paper and Google into a verb for Internet searching. It is the customer, looking for a co-op or condo, perhaps, who equates Donald Trump, the world's most famous real estate developer, with luxury real estate and a luxurious lifestyle overall, and is willing to pay more to live in a building that carries the Trump name. If customers can be convinced that your product is distinctly different from and better than your competitors, they will be willing to pay more for your product or service, and that's a very special, enviable situation.

When that happens for you, you're in a protected position. It's not because you can legally prevent others from inventing pain relievers, tissues, copiers, search engines or building luxury real estate with the same basic materials, but because customers will choose your product over others, even though rivals may strive to emulate you. That's why, for example, Google has become the most popular Internet brand, according to a Jupiter Research survey, followed (but not all that closely) by Yahoo, Amazon and eBay. Google, valued at $202 billion, is now considered the fourth most valuable technology company after Apple, Microsoft, and IBM valued at $258 billion, which has also been around much longer.

WHEN A PATENT CAN BE A DISADVANTAGE

Filing for a patent with the U.S. Patent and Trademark Office is time-consuming — it takes about two years from filing date to processing. It's also expensive, especially if you seek international rights, not just the U.S. rights. Besides time and cost, another disadvantage of patenting your product or idea is that you need to disclose exactly how it works. Of course, the concept behind patents is that in exchange you are granted a monopoly, for a fixed number or years, to own the rights to your invention and its revenues. After that time is up, you will have relinquished those rights, and other companies are free to make and sell a similar product without paying you.

However, there is a far cheaper and faster method than patenting. It is called "defensive publishing." This means publishing a description of your innovation, for example on a Website such as www.IPworld.com in technology, or in a trade journal, newsletter or bulletin. This strategy is meant to prevent competitors from getting a patent for the same idea. Patent lawyers call this "prior art." It's becoming more common among big corporations as well as smaller companies. These companies are finding that the potential risk in putting your innovation out in the public domain pales compared to the advantage of staking a claim as its originator, blocking others from patenting it, and giving you the right to obtain licensing fees from potential users.

By the way, patents have been granted not only for products but also for business processes, such as one-click shopping on retailer websites. However, it's now become harder to get a patent on a new product that combines elements of existing patents, thanks to a new test the U.S. Supreme Court established in April of 2007.

Technology has a long history of brilliant innovations that weren't patented but resulted from "open source" software. This is a form of licensing that gives licenses outright without the licensee retaining ownership, in order to share the idea with the public for altruistic reasons. The non-profit Open Source Initiative invented a development method for software that ensures collaborative peer review and a transparent process. Was anything significant invented thanks to open sourcing? Well yes! Among others, no less than the original Netscape Internet browser that grew out of Mosaic and the Linux Operating System.

One of my former companies was sold to a much larger entity, even though we possessed no technology patents, but instead had developed a large amount of proprietary software, which was protected by virtue of copyright.

COPYRIGHTS: DEBUNKING MYTHS

Speaking of copyrights, did you know that ideas, processes, methods, systems and devices are not protected by copyright in the U.S.? Neither are mere listings of ingredients or contents, or titles, names, slogans and short phrases, according to the U.S. Copyright Office. What is protected? Literary, visual, musical, film, architectural or performing arts-related "original works of authorship;" in other words, execution based on the idea.

Because authorship begins when the work is created and a "copy" is fixed for the first time, no registration or other action in the Copyright Office is required. Nonetheless, there are advantages to registering your copyright of an eligible work if any infringement on your authorship is expected and you care about defending it. In case of infringement, you may win higher monetary damages in court if a copyright is registered for your work.

TRADEMARKS: A DISTINCTIVE LOOK FOR YOUR PRODUCT

A trademark is a distinctive sign or mark used by a business or individual that uniquely identifies some of its products or services and differentiates it from others. A trademark is typically a logo, design, name or phrase. Like copyrights, registering a trademark is not required by the U.S. Patent and Trademark Office. But the owner of a registered trademark can sue for infringement to bar unauthorized use of the trademark, as it's then regarded as a form of property.

Courts have sometimes ruled that trademarks are generic and thus no longer apply, as happened with Bayer's "aspirin," meaning that other companies were free to use that name for "acetylsalicylic acid" (and you can see why so many others did). Xerox, however, retains its trademark for copier machines and defends it.

FOCUS ON YOUR CUSTOMER, NOT ON YOUR PRODUCT

An inventor/ founder/ CEO's focus should be squarely on the customer — the end user of the product or idea. This means determining how to reach that customer, roughly how much to spend to reach the customer, the best distribution channels, and so on. Whether you seek to reach Internet users, cancer patients, parents of small children, frequent business travelers, or buyers of homes costing $2 million and up, your customer should drive the above decisions more than your actual product does. I think the reasons are obvious, but too many inventors develop a sort of myopia about their product idea. This is understandable, given the hundreds of hours and intense concentration required to create it, but this is often not very helpful in protecting the product and in bringing it to market.

THE INNOVATOR'S DILEMMA

No one works in isolation. Even those who truly think they are lone wolves, such as writers or artists, need others, including agents, editors, publishers and publicists, to bring their creative work to the public. This is true for any innovator. When you share information about your invention or idea, it's natural to worry about how to protect it. Sometimes paranoia sets in and innovators become preoccupied with people "stealing" their idea.

Actually, talking to others about your idea is one way to find out how unique it is, and how much demand may exist for it. People almost always overestimate what someone will do with your idea if they "steal" it. If you are so fearful of sharing information that you feel your idea would lose all value if someone heard about it, well, then, maybe it's not so valuable after all. For your idea to be successful, you need a team to work on it, perfect it and bring it to market. I know from experience that this collaborative effort is as important as the idea itself. Without a team behind it, your idea will be stillborn. Of course you want to protect your idea, but not at the cost of not building a team — that's way too high a cost!

ASHMEET'S POINTS TO REMEMBER

- It is hard for others to "steal" your idea. Avoid paranoia.
- Patents are not the be-all, do-all, end-all for many businesses.
- Building a team is vitally important.
- Focus on the customer.
- March to a different drummer when it comes to your business model.

One last thing: I call it my First Law: an entrepreneur should seriously consider the first offer. There is a high likelihood that there will never be another reasonable offer, let alone a better one. Take the additional time, risk, capital and other factors into account and, only if you have a lot of conviction backed up with cold hard analysis should you NOT take the money. Every time I have gone against this advice, I have regretted it!

"Sometimes you're the windshield; sometimes you're the bug."

— MARK KNOPFLER (1949 –)
SCOTTISH MUSICIAN,
CO-FOUNDER OF DIRE STRAITS

4

A BATTLED-SCARRED WARRIOR SHARES HIS ROAD-SHOW LESSONS LEARNED

IF YOU ARE AN ENTREPRENEUR who wants to build a business structure around your invention, innovation, product, new drug, new use of an old drug, new type of medical instrument, new technology or whatever, you will need to raise capital. Like it or not, this imperative comes with the territory. Someone has to go out and ask for money — go "on the road" both literally and figuratively.

Starting a new venture is like running a marathon. You start out well rested, raring to go. As time passes, you begin to fatigue. No rest for the weary — the long road to the finish line still stretches ahead. Those qualified investors are the ones who will hand you water to rehydrate you as you pass by; they are the ones cheering you on, because by investing with you and in you they are expressing their belief that you will "win the race" and want to help you keep running forward until you finally cross the finish line.

With your passion and determination to build your little company into one that you hope will take off — go public, help treat some devastating disease or otherwise "fly into the clouds" — you may initially pay the bills by bootstrapping, as so do many other CEOs, inventors, innovators and entrepreneurs. That can mean maxing out credit cards, taking a second mortgage on your home, going hat in hand to friends and family, shamelessly working your extended personal contacts, perhaps bringing in a partner or partners who likewise do not have the deepest pockets but can contribute, giving them a share of what is essentially a shared conviction that you are truly "on to something big."

At first this will help; it will get you off the ground, take you a certain distance. But at some point, and usually sooner rather than later, you are going to need enough "fuel" for a much longer trip from professional investors.

The sad truth is, if you don't need money, plenty of people will want to lend it to you. Raising capital for a new venture is actually the hardest thing in the world to do. Along the way you will encounter all kinds of characters, and some of those saints — and monsters — I encountered are profiled here. The armor you need includes patience, resilience and, most of all, a sense of humor. The one predictable thing I discovered is that you can never predict where your investors will come from. People you expect to invest won't and those you don't expect to will often surprise you by actually investing. That means you have to bring your "A game" to every meeting.

These are a few of my lessons learned about how to tell when you might be wasting your time. Hopefully these may spare you the accompanying angst I experienced.

LESSON: VENTURE CAPITALISTS ARE NOT ALWAYS INVINCIBLE...

After founding Urigen (described in next chapter) we did have several angels invest with us. This was very helpful at the outset. As things progressed, we were still reliant on protracted fundraising to advance the company — a process that took almost two years.

Once we put it out there that we were open to traditional venture financing, one venture capital group sent a person to visit our scientific founder's clinic. They told me in advance that if they were to invest, this was the person who would replace me as CEO of the company that I founded. At one point in his visit, the would-be CEO got upset by what he thought was a lot of blood on a cart. Anyone in the medical field could have told him that the "blood" was Betadine®, a topical disinfectant you can buy in a drugstore. This was a guy who was supposed to be much more experienced and just plain smarter than the rest of us.

Interestingly, we learned that these particular venture capitalists were enamored at that time with an academic largely because her husband had a private jet. We guessed that they may have spent the better part of $1 million incubating her technology, which we had recognized as a non-starter after we did a 30-minute cursory review of it.

At the end, this venture capital company wrote a proposal that valued us at about $400,000. Several weeks later the head of the company asked me to meet him on the weekend for coffee. When I politely disputed his valuation, he proceeded to insult me, saying that I must never have done a deal. Although I really needed to have the resources of that (or any!) venture firm at that stage of our development, I also knew the only way for it to make sense for us, and provide a return, was to go out and raise capital on the road. That's what we did, even though, as I said, it took about two years. And contrary to what this VC believed, it turned out we were worthy — at a valuation of approximately $5 million! Okay, so I'm already contradicting the "First Law" in my last chapter — the one about taking the first offer. Let me revise that: Don't take the first offer if it comes from a jerk.

LESSON: ALWAYS DO DUE DILIGENCE FIRST BEFORE SETTING UP A NEW MEETING, AND ALWAYS BREAK IN YOUR NEW SHOES

I had plans to be in Milan to meet with a potential partner for Urigen's lead program in Italy. I always travel light, so I had only one pair of shoes, a new pair. That was a bad mistake. On the first day of my trip, I discovered they did not fit. However, I had 18-hour days booked for over a week. What I remember most is making it to the parking lot of the hotel, taking my shoes off, and seeing that my feet were rubbed raw and my socks were bloody. So much for giving your all for the company!

Before I flew to Milan, I was contacted by a potential investor's office in Switzerland. The investor wanted to meet me in Milan. As I had other business there, I agreed to a meeting. Two gentlemen arrived and wanted to see my I.D. I showed them my passport but they did not want me to see theirs. Eventually, one of them showed me a Norwegian passport with a name that seemed Arabic. The other offered a business card where he had literally scratched off all of the contact information, including the address, phone and e-mail. He explained that they had all expired.

Mind you, this meeting in Italy was taking place in German. After about 30 minutes we agreed that my German, even with all the pointing and gesturing, was not sufficient to understand one another. So the next day they arrived with their "secretary," who spoke English. They really didn't seem too interested in our technology, which was, in fact, genuinely exciting, and asked for a return of seven percent, annually, to be personally guaranteed. During our discussions, the "secretary" let it slip that she had just met them on the street that day. So much for their funding the entire round, which their colleague in Zurich had said might be in the cards.

LESSON: YOU CAN BE HUMBLED IN YOUR OWN HOMETOWN

One of my company's ventures is a company called "Inverseon" for lung diseases. The initial capital for the first Inverseon clinical trial came from the state of Kansas. After waiting almost six hours for my opportunity to speak, while listening to other pitches — for special wheels for tractors and the like — I had to describe the most complicated concept I have ever encountered in pharmacology. Almost unbelievably, we did get the money and the clinical trial worked so well that it was covered in the prestigious medical journal, *The Lancet* (BJ Lipworth, PA Williamson. Vol. 373, 104–5, Jan. 10, 2009).

However, on several other occasions in my hometown I was not so lucky. At an event for angel investors, I was standing at one of those little tables and noticed that the company presenting at one table over had developed special sunglasses for golfers. An investor walked up and spoke with them for about five minutes and, as I watched, wrote them a check on the spot for $50,000. I told the investor what we were doing in drug development and he just turned around and walked away. Yet another time in Kansas I was equally humbled: we were at a Wichita conference waiting for our turn when we were told at the last minute that we were not going to be allowed to present our pitch at all. It turned out that another company had been allowed to replace us — and did get funded — with an important device that holds your socks together in the dryer!

LESSON: WHENEVER POSSIBLE, ALSO DO DUE DILIGENCE ON INDIVIDUALS

We had $500 in the bank and had flown to Europe on our credit cards to present to one of the largest foundations in the world. This was after one year of negotiations for what looked like a potential investment of about $5 million. This was actually our second trip to Europe for these investors. At the final presentation, the lead outside consultant questioner looked at his notes, refused to read our slides, and said that he simply did not believe the data we presented. We later learned that this individual — whose name we did not have in advance, so we were not able to look him up — makes $400,000 per year as consultant to a competitive company that our product threatens.

Being on the road is exhausting and, as you can see, it is a numbers game and in some ways a "trial by endurance." At times I was so tired from jet lag that I was not always immediately sure what country I was in. I have done road shows where I presented a Power Point and slides while virtually asleep. Fortunately, no one else noticed, since I really knew my material and could speak to the slides by rote. However, I did have to be a lot more awake for the Q&As.

Over the years I have gotten lost in foreign cities, dealt with angry cab drivers and, in many instances, deeply regretted my lack of foreign language skills. The day I realized that I need reading glasses was when I found myself standing in the rain in Germany looking at a posted map and could not see the street name I needed.

I have been ignored, insulted, refused and often bemused by the reception we received, when I know in my heart that what my team has to offer is so much more important to the human race than special golf glasses. Holding your socks together in the dryer...well, that perhaps is of significance. One sock does always seem to disappear.

What does not and will not disappear for me, and I hope this holds true for you, too, is my ironclad determination to find investors who share my vision. In the long run, despite these "detours," I have been successful in finding those insightful investors, including angels and some institutional investors, and you will too. Just keep moving forward, and always remember the words of Rudyard Kipling:

> *"If you can keep your head when all about you*
> *Are losing theirs and blaming it on you*
> *... you'll be a Man my son!"*
> (FROM KIPLING'S POEM "IF.")

MORE GARNER'S RULES OF THE ROAD

- VCs don't finance most deals; it is up to you to find other ways.
- File at least one grant application to focus your thinking.
- You're a fundraiser; don't be ashamed to beg,
- You can never predict where your investors will come from.
- Research your prospective investors before meetings, if possible.
- Nurture your sense of humor — you'll need it.
- It is all about the people.

Now let me tell you about Urigen...

"Far and away, the best prize that life offers
is the chance to work hard at work worth doing."

— THEODORE ROOSEVELT

5

URIGEN PHARMACEUTICAL'S URGENTLY NEEDED TREATMENT

INTERSTITIAL CYSTITIS, OR PAINFUL BLADDER SYNDROME (IC/PBS), is a recognized medical condition. In North America today, there are conservatively an estimated 10.5 million women and men who suffer from IC/PBS. The condition is characterized by bladder pain, urinary urgency and frequency as well as interrupted sleep and even bedwetting. The shocking fact is that few IC treatments exist and no approved therapies are available for IC/PBS. Some people are in such constant pain that they contemplate suicide.

I founded Urigen Pharmaceuticals after a visit to the urology clinic run by Dr. Lowell Parsons, who was also a professor and Director of the Division of Urology at the University of California at San Diego. He had given me a rundown on the problems and challenges. It was when I met with several of his patients and heard their stories that I became fully aware of how these people were suffering in silence, how much under-diagnosis or full-out misdiagnosis exists in this arena, and how Dr. Parsons could turn this entire picture around for millions of people.

Among the patient's stories I heard was this one from a businessman. His name is changed to protect his privacy, but his story is real. "Ralph Tisdale" wanted to die. For almost a decade, Tisdale, now 64, found the unremitting pain and urgent feeling that he needed to urinate at least 20 times a day more than an inconvenience. For years Tisdale lived a lie, telling no one except the parade of doctors he consulted what he was going through.

His marriage failed, his life was becoming more miserable with each passing day, and his comment was, "How do you tell people your penis hurts? That it was a big factor in my divorce. This affliction was controlling my life, so I made excuses at meetings, at dinners — I have to make a call, I have to blow my nose, I need a smoke." (Ralph doesn't smoke).

"I can even stand to tell this embarrassing story now," he says. "I was in an airplane, stuck on the runway, and they told us we'd have to stay in our seats. I had gone to the men's room before we got on the plane, but now I had to go again, so badly that it was either they shut off the engines or I would urinate in my seat. So they shut the plane down. I can still feel the humiliation of walking down that aisle, but what could I do? The urologists I went to tried really hard, but they had nothing for me. Then, thank God, I found Dr. Parsons, and the new treatment he helped create." Today, Tisdale reports, "I can drive for nine hours straight, as I did recently, and not have to stop once." He is pain free — and although not "cured" he definitely has his life back. He is also seeing someone and hopes to remarry. "Nobody should have to suffer the way I did!" he told me.

This story and ones like it brought me together with Dr. Lowell Parsons and the small public specialty pharmaceutical company we built and named Urigen Pharmaceuticals. This company is dedicated to the development and commercialization of therapeutic products for urological disorders with a hopeful ending for millions of sufferers who have nowhere else to turn. Urigen's URG101 is a proprietary pharmaceutical treatment comprised of lidocaine and heparin.

Almost 70% of those with IC/PBS are women. Another patient I spoke with was Georgia resident "Tina," now age 36, a human resources executive, who first experienced symptoms when she was 20. Like Ralph Tisdale and so many others, Tina also had to endure a decade of horror before she took part in a clinical trial, was treated with UGR101, and got relief. "From the very first treatment, it felt like a miracle. It still does," she says. Her trial was presided over by another urologist who participated in the clinical trial, Dr. Jeffrey Proctor, at his private practice, Georgia Urology PA, outside Atlanta.

"I felt like I had to urinate constantly. I also had chronic pelvic pain and frequent leakage," Tina told me, "I would get up from my computer and there would be a small puddle in the chair." She had consulted several urologists and over the years had been prescribed all kinds of drugs, alone and in combination. Nothing helped. "After a really painful cystoscopy, they found lesions on my bladder. They don't know yet what causes them, but I was told the mucus membrane of my bladder was deteriorated. Still, knowing this didn't help my symptoms and things went from bad to worse. I went online, to chat rooms full of other people who were also desperate for help. Finally someone told me about Dr. Jeffrey Proctor. The day I saw him, my pain was a 10, the worst ever, but it was also my lucky day. He put me right into his clinical trial and I got URG101. The difference was amazing, almost immediately. That night, for the first time in years, I slept through the night. For the next two to three weeks, the pain, the urge to urinate all the time, and the leaking, were 90% gone. Now I'm a new woman."

The disease does not discriminate by age, gender or ethnicity. "Anne," a bright, brown-eyed seventh grader, now lives the fun-filled life of a normal fourteen-year-old girl. But just a few years ago Anne was wearing "pull-up" diapers and was in the same extreme pain that both Ralph and Tina described. As Drs. Parson and Proctor relate, although it is underreported, this condition is much more prevalent in children than supposed. Dr. Parsons now has 75 children with this condition under his care. Anne's condition was so bad that at one point, as her parents reported, "The doctors wanted to remove her bladder, which they told us was the most inflamed bladder they had ever seen. She would have had to have an ileostomy and perhaps wear a colostomy bag forever. Imagine our relief to find this new drug!"

As I learned how severely this condition affected men, women and children, along with their concentric circles of loved ones and colleagues, all of whom suffer because their loved ones suffer, I decided that this was a condition that deserved to be attended to, in order to give these people the relief they so urgently want, need and deserve.

FOUNDING URIGEN

When I worked briefly at Roche Laboratories, the U.S. pharmaceutical business of the Swiss company, we had an oral chemotherapeutic,

Xeloda®, which had just been approved on phase II data. Xeloda® is an oral drug, which did not allow for the same levels of reimbursement as a drug given by infusion via an intravenous line. In fact, the route of administration may determine reimbursement, and therefore the viability of a product. That brings me back to what happened years later, when I was visiting the clinic run by Dr. Parsons. I witnessed his treating patients with a drug given by installation into the urinary bladder. When he told me that there was existing reimbursement for these procedures, it definitely increased my interest in licensing his technology.

Most of us start any new venture with finite resources, and I was no exception. At my company's formation stage I, like many others, could not afford expensive market research, which can run to hundreds of thousands of dollars. But sometimes all it takes are a few well-conceived questions to get the feedback you need. For example, when I wanted to do my initial due diligence (which I call my "Kansas City Due Diligence") on this new biotech venture with Dr. Parsons, I went directly to the doctors' lunchroom at the community hospital where my father, my sister and my brother-in-law all practice medicine and surgery.

I sat there talking with my father, who is an orthopedic surgeon and inventor, and my sister, an ophthalmologist. Just then a busy OB/GYN walked in for a quick bite. When questioned, this doctor told me that, yes, there are a significant number of patients with the type of bladder pain Urigen would ultimately seek to treat. She also confirmed that the treatment options for these patients are extremely limited. Voila! People really needed our treatment. That's how I knew I was on the right track with my sophisticated market research. This began an eight-year odyssey that survived two international relocations.

When people think of initial public offerings, IPOs, they often think of working with a rather established, maybe even household name investment bank, raising potentially hundreds of millions of dollars. Yet entrepreneurs in finance and in innovation-dependent industries like high tech, specialty pharmaceuticals and biotech have developed creative business models for some time. One thing that people sometimes do is take advantage of the opportunity to merge a private company into an already-public company where its main business, for example, might be dying (or dead) due to some practical issue. This is called a reverse merger. That was the case with Urigen.

As entrepreneurs, we look for different sources of financing and I found a company that had been in the biotech industry and had raised quite a lot of money, gone public, had thousands of shareholders and then decided they were going to seek strategic alternatives. I cold-called them, literally. This time my call was to their Chairman and CEO on a weekend, and he called back. Over a period of time, we merged the companies, and the resulting entity went public under its new name.

In speculative industries like mining and biopharmaceuticals, there are also smaller stock exchanges around the world — in places like Canada, Australia, Hong Kong, and the alternative investment market in London — that have attracted a lot of small IPOs and reverse merger companies like Urigen. Entrepreneurs look for opportunities and do what they need to do. This is one strategy, certainly one that is employed more and more. Once you've gone public, you have access to capital that you wouldn't have had access to as a private company. You have a stock or a currency you can then use to finance a strategic acquisition or build a business faster.

Urigen concentrated upon products and therapies that would be useful to urologists and gynecologists. As the reverse merger was progressing, our clinical trial results came in; to our great surprise and disappointment, the study did not work. We still believed in what we were doing, but were now essentially out of money and had to somehow find a way forward. I still remember the feel of the table on which my hands were pressing down when I heard those results. I closed my eyes and put my head down on the table, but just for a moment. I took a deep breath, stood fully upright and realized that I had to go tell our merger partner. I drove over to their offices later that day and convinced them to continue with the transaction.

We did complete the transaction, went public and raised our first real institutional capital. We also, of course, carefully reviewed the study and identified several issues that needed correcting. When we reran the study, it achieved statistical significance on all end points. We had originally outsourced much of the work to a clinical research organization and they essentially had run the study too quickly.

We were able to go back to the drawing board, and in about a year Urigen Pharmaceuticals (www.urigen.com) announced results of its phase II multi-center, double-blind, placebo-controlled, crossover-designed clinical trial of URG101 in patients with Interstitial Cystitis/Painful Bladder Syndrome (IC/PBS). The drug was found to significantly reduce painful bladder syndrome or interstitial cystitis symptoms following a single dose! This was the most exciting result in a double-blind, placebo-controlled, multi-center study in this area in over a decade. The primary endpoint was statistically significant, as were all the secondary endpoints! Before I left the company in 2010, Dr. Parsons and I recruited an executive to complete the pivotal trials of URG101. Certainly the final chapter of Urigen's story has yet to be told but the progress is most heartening.

Caring physicians and nurses who treat them work tirelessly to help patients, but what is often missed is the key role entrepreneurs play in changing lives. I believe the Urigen example, and the story that follows, are instructive in highlighting how this partnership can make such a critical difference.

STILL MORE GARNER RULES OF THE ROAD

- You can have a public company on a smaller exchange.
- Market research can be done with your existing resources.
- Getting to know your customers can be a powerful driver for the hard road ahead.
- Try to discover as many of your end product's revenue sources as you can.
- To go public, look for alternatives, such as doing a reverse merger with an established company.
- Don't accept a setback without a careful review of what happened.

"The test of success is not what you do when you're on top.
Success is how high you bounce when you hit bottom."

— GENERAL GEORGE S. PATTON

6

WHY INVERSEON'S UPHILL STRUGGLE FOR A GREAT CAUSE MAY FEEL FAMILIAR

IN THE EARLY 2000S, my firm, EGB Advisors, began working with the MD Anderson Cancer Center to help augment their licensing efforts, and we set up what was essentially a West Coast branch of their office. I was also spending three or four days a month in Houston working directly out of the Center's Office of Technology Commercialization.

One evening, after a full day at MD Anderson, I went over to the University of Houston to meet with Professor Richard Bond, Ph.D. I'd been told that Dr. Bond was one of the most creative professors in the area. Richard explained how he had risked his career to move into a field brand new to him — respiratory disease. I liked him from that first meeting and decided on the spot to work with him to form a company.

Over twenty million Americans suffer from asthma and related respiratory conditions. The potential market was never in question. His work involved using beta-blockers to relieve asthmatics of their debilitating symptoms. He also came to believe that this approach could improve treatment for many other chronic diseases, both in respiratory conditions and other chronic diseases. As someone energized by challenges, this was particularly exciting to me, since he was proposing to use drugs in precisely the indications where they were not to be used, or in medical terms, contraindicated!

Richard Bond had essentially asked himself this question: "If you have a chronic disease, do you care what a drug does for a day or two, or do you care what that drug can do for you over weeks, months and years?" Obviously with chronic situations the latter predominates, and this is exactly the pharmacological approach that Bond used to examine the body's response. He had done some theoretical work on how the body's receptors acted, and he was criticized for not having prior animal test data. He did then develop animal data, only to face questions about how this might work with humans. We helped him move into a series of formal human clinical trials.

With Inverseon's technology rights, as with DelMar, we took a divergent path from the norm. The university assigned (in other words, gave) the initial intellectual property to Professor Bond. In exchange all he had to do was share ten percent of the stock in the company that we had given him. Over time we have jointly worked on four grants, which have put more money back into the university than a traditional license might have. This arrangement allowed us the freedom to advance the technology, using best industry practices, without having to deal with a stifling license arrangement.

Negotiating with the university to assign the intellectual property to our new company took almost a year, during which we had to walk away several times. We do credit the forward thinking of the administration at the University of Houston for working with us to make this project happen.

The insights we have had, and continue to have, thanks to our collaboration with Dr. Bond, could also lead to novel treatments of diseases of the central nervous system, including diabetes and other chronic conditions. This true synergy — a good omen for a fruitful partnership — is what researchers and investors should always look for.

FALSE STARTS THAT MAY STRIKE A FAMILIAR CORD

At one point, Richard got us before several board members at one of the nation's top three pharmaceutical companies. He gave a tour de force presentation, which was so well received and got them so excited, that they offered us a term sheet on the spot. We quickly worked on it at our end and had an agreement, but one not yet formalized. A few days later, our champion was on the front page of *The Wall Street Journal* — not the place I wanted to see his likeness at this stage. He had just left for a huge new position in health care. It was an exciting and positive move for him, but as it turned out, a huge negative for us. Our main relationship had been with this individual, and without another enthusiastic champion shepherding this through, it just died.

Next we were up for a large grant from the National Institute of Health (NIH), which we felt confident we had a solid 80% to 90% chance of getting. That grant never materialized. In Chapter Four I also described an incident from this same time period, when we had been told we were in line for a multimillion-dollar investment from one of the largest charities in Europe. After a year of back and forth communication with them, making trips to Europe at our own expense, practicing our elevator pitch, perfecting our Power Points, and strategizing — not to mention a year of continuous phone calls and e-mails — we flew in to make our the final presentation. The charity's consultant, a man I had never met, did not even want to see our slides. He read from a prepared statement that he essentially did not believe our results. I thought beliefs were for religious services and not scientific proceedings! Needless to say, they vetoed the investment, and that was it for us. As I also said earlier, this man had a conflict of interest, since he was also consulting for a competitor whose multibillion-dollar franchise is threatened by our program.

Another time, the red flag was visible right away. A banker in New York put a deal together for Inverseon with a public company but we just could not get over the fact that, in a company with three employees, the CEO had both a driver and an assistant! This did not bode well and we knew we had to let this "deal" go.

In another dead end, we were in discussions with a private company that had a public listing in the works for one of their small public companies. They suggested we structure a deal in which we would be financed concurrently by backing into their company through a reverse merger arrangement. We agreed. However, their investors decided not to move forward and soon after they all lost their entire investments in this company. These experiences just show how eager and open we were to doing anything that could get our venture off the ground and closer to the finish line.

FINALLY, RECOGNITION OF INVERSEON'S POTENTIAL

Interspersed with these tales of woe there have also been some great, encouraging moments. One day, long after we had forgotten about two government grant applications we had written, one of my Inverseon and EGB partners, Amie Franklin, Ph.D, got a call about these grants. She was told that the money had been available for months, and that if we wanted it, we had better log into our account. You can be sure Amie did just that, with no hesitation!

In another development, in 2009, in Vienna, at the largest pulmonary meeting in the world, a special symposium was set up solely to discuss our work. Almost 1,000 people attended. There were speakers pro and con about what we were doing, but as the sessions progressed, many audience members began to react supportively. Finally, people were paying attention!

Soon we began our move into new lead indications in the areas of smoking cessation and chronic bronchitis. In 2010, Inverseon recruited Mitchell Glass, MD. As a pulmonologist who had also developed an important clinical strategy as part of the development of a cardiovascular drug, Mitchell's background was perfect for us. The drug he worked on developing was actually the model for our own drug development. In fact, Mitchell had started in drug development at Imperial Chemical Industries (ICI), where he worked with the renowned Sir James Black, who had developed beta-blockers, like propranolol, and H-2 blockers such as Tagamet®.

Over the years, Mitchell Glass and his teams have received five drug approvals, including approvals for innovative pulmonary medications. After a careful review of all of *our* data, he refined our development plans and brought them to an even higher level. Brilliant and meticulous, he saw the bigger picture, understood all the government rules and regulations, and repositioned our lead indication as smoking cessation, with a target of filing for marketing approval in as soon as three years. Previously our lead indication was asthma. Glass reprioritized them as: One, Smoking Cessation; Two, Chronic Bronchitis; Three, Cystic Fibrosis; and Four, Asthma. Among the several major advantages of this refocus were that less capital was required, and that there was now a more direct path to market through the FDA.

In 2010, all of our hard work began to pay off, and all of the false starts and disappointments faded into the background, like the forgotten labor pains of childbirth when you hold your child. That year the Chair of an FDA Advisory Panel stated that he believes our approach may replace an entire class of respiratory drugs for certain indications. His favorable comments about our work were published in *BioCentury*. The complete article is on www.EGBadvisors.com. Since the drugs he referenced as comparisons have sales second only to statin drugs such as Lipitor® you can imagine our elation.

Even with this encouragement, the reality is that nothing in this arena happens quickly. There is more to be done, but the work is progressing nicely. Currently two additional clinical studies are planned at major teaching hospitals across the country. Thanks to the results thus far, we are more than a little optimistic that we will be able to take our drug to market in the not too distant future!

GARNER'S RULES OF THE ROAD (CONTINUED)

- It is worth reiterating that the team is essential.
- Hone your arguments that universities can and need to be flexible in working with entrepreneurs.
- Looking on the university as a partner and acting like one yourself results in benefits for both.
- Researchers and investors should look for the widest range of applications for their product or technology.
- Expect to spend months, even years, to negotiate the best terms for your company.
- Don't forget to follow up on your grant applications!

"Take a chance! All life is a chance. The man who goes the furthest is generally the one who is willing to do and dare. The 'sure thing' boat never gets far from shore."

— DALE CARNEGIE

7

CREATING THE INNOVATION ANGEL CARD TO HELP FUND START-UPS

ABOUT FIVE YEARS AGO, in the early stages of trying to fund both Urigen and Inverseon, my partners and I found ourselves deeply dissatisfied with the nature of the funding offers we had received, and especially frustrated by the red tape that always seems to follow small business technology transfer research grants (also known as STTRs).

One day, I attended a talk given by a man named David Thomson, who was once the subject of an article in *Investor's Business Daily* under the headline "Management Guru uncovers patterns behind billion-dollar firms." The talk centered on the core concepts in his book, *Blueprint to a Billion*. Thomson suggested that if a person was going to try for a small slice of an established market, it might make more sense, rather than go down that path, to try to create a new market.

Easier said than done, of course, but it got me thinking. Eventually I came up with the idea of combining angel investing with credit card rewards. The original concept came to me one day when I found myself doing everyday things such as buying a cup of coffee, going to a movie, and filling my car with gas. Invariably I paid for these and other goods and services with my credit card.

Most credit cards have small bonuses that accrue from their regular use. These bonuses may take the form of cash rebates, frequent flyer miles or discounted goods or services. They also function as a psychological bond between the consumer and the card-issuing partner.

Yes, I was accumulating points with my purchases, but points for what? To get a free airline flight only after having racked up 25,000 to 50,000 miles, or to purchase some other item I could afford to buy and didn't really need points to pay for them? The benefits derived from these points were marginal at best for me, and likely many others felt the same.

Might there be a way, I asked myself, to repurpose these points to a more socially-relevant and satisfying end? Could they, for example, be turned into instruments to stimulate innovation, and perhaps in some way help transcend the localized nature of most angel investments? Most importantly, could points generated by credit card transactions be used to fund ways to expand product research and ways to use such research in pharmaceuticals and other areas? In other words, could these points potential serve great human needs by providing urgently needed funding?

These random musings began to coalesce into what I thought was an interesting concept. I called my new idea the "Angel Investor Card" (AIC). The idea of an AIC, as you can see, was to merge the phenomenon of angel investing with the well-established business practice of affinity marketing via credit cards.

My original idea was to design this card not for the masses but specifically for potential angel investors, individuals who have a high net worth and superior credit. There are an estimated two million plus individuals in the United States who have an annual income exceeding $250,000. These more affluent individuals would apply to the sponsoring financial institution (bank) for this special credit card. Once approved, they would use that card for their purchases. A portion of the purchase price of each item or service they paid for with this card would be siphoned off to a pre-designated investment fund. When that fund reached a certain critical mass, it would be invested in the targeted innovation. The cardholder would get monthly statements or could go online to review the progress of the investment fund or funds in which they were now invested. They would also have an option to "up the ante" by adding additional amounts of money to the funds they had designated.

Because of the very different payoff of this nontraditional affinity card program, I thought it could be more attractive to angel investors, who already have some established wealth and are hardly in need of small discounts or additional frequent flyer miles. Angel Investor Card members would choose an area of research or innovation of interest to them, and could also contribute to funding that area through the cash-back portion of each transaction. This would give the participant a number of advantages, the most attractive of which would be early access to breakthrough opportunities. They would also get the psychological satisfaction of being able to direct their investment into an area they found socially meaningful. For instance, an angel investor whose father had passed away from prostate cancer could dedicate his invested funds to researchers who were developing an early detection test, or those who were working on finding a cure for this dread disease. As the company grew, went public and achieved liquidity, the angel investor would get a return commensurate with the amount of his or her investment.

My expectation for this idea, which did follow David Thomson's sage if not always easy to achieve advice to "create a new market," was that participation would appeal to this subgroup of credit card holders who were already angel investors or had an interest in becoming such investors. This card, I reasoned, becoming more excited about my idea day by day, would turn every investor into a miniature portfolio manager, able to prioritize his investments in ways that are not possible through conventional managed funds. It would also require no minimum investment amount, and the monies accumulated through the AIC programs would not be subject to expiration, as frequent flyer miles often are. It would also immediately grant them membership in a prescreened, exclusive group.

I knew that for the Angel Investor Card to make a proper "splash" in the financial services industry and achieve rapid market penetration it would need to partner with a major financial institution, specifically a bank that issues credit cards, the larger the better. Since this financial institution would already be familiar with the details of managing and tracking affinity credit card programs, this would also present them with another way to generate revenue without a major overhaul of their back-office systems.

To bring this idea to life, I began by first recruiting colleagues with an international marketing background to partner with me. Together we filed the business process patent and began work. I also recruited two other colleagues to join us: a credit card veteran as well as an information technology expert. Our merry band was ready. We researched and made a short but powerful list of potential card issuers — just as the economy was tanking.

Undaunted at first, we called a bank in Wichita and, unable to reach the highest executive, tried to explain to a secretary what an angel investor is. We also called a bank in Puerto Rico. Working our way up from the *bottom* of our list, trying to hone our pitch, we finally did get a bite from a bank and had a term sheet, which of course was pending legal due diligence by the issuer's legal department.

Meanwhile, we went to law firm after law firm ourselves, to have them structure an entity that would allow us to create securities with the cash that potential card members would be converting into our proposed angel investment fund. These firms were taking our money and not providing any helpful structures. Then one of my colleagues who had joined our team — he was an expert in international marketing and therefore very important to our project — called and told me sadly that he might be very sick. He, in fact, had a deadly form of cancer and was gone in about five months.

After a deep breath, I assembled a new team. We recognized that we would need to raise $2 million just for the legal and accounting fees required under existing U.S. securities laws. Despite the encouragement we got from a promising institutional investor, who called me and said this was one of the best deals he had ever seen — and he sees over 600 deals a year — we did not have the necessary funds, and actually over time came to the realization that our original business model of using the cash back to buy stock in start-ups was not viable. Nonetheless we still believed we were on to "the next big thing" and were still determined to find another way to make this card happen.

Since then we have changed the name from Angel Investor Card to Innovation Angel Card. Now the card member's benefit is no longer his or her investment but rather a tax credit. Instead of shares in an innovative new company, credit card members would receive a tax benefit for helping to support innovative companies.

We have formed a not-for-profit in California and have applied for 501(c)3 status at the federal level: www.innovationangelcard.org. We still believe we have something special and remain eager to give it the time and attention it deserves and fulfill our vision for its future.

Don't you think that about your venture too — at least most of the time?

Making the leap from chalkboard to store shelf can be torturous. We all need encouragement about our ventures, *and* the dollars needed to do it. I hope I have given *you* hope...and perhaps some useful advice along the way.

In the resounding words of Samuel Beckett: "Fail. Fail again. Fail better." Or perhaps a better quote to end this book on for you, my fellow intrepid seekers, are these words, which echo down the ages:

"Wheresoever you go, go with all your heart."
— CONFUCIUS

Whether you are the person in the lab coat, the entrepreneurial CEO, or a person with cash who wants to track down promising research that can make that big leap, I would love to connect and hear what you are up to. Let's talk!

Meantime, thanks for taking this journey with me, and good luck with yours.

FINAL RULES OF THE ROAD FROM BILL GARNER

- Raising money for your venture is a never-ending challenge.
- Instead of aiming for a small slice of an established market, think of creating a new market.
- Before spending a lot of money on attorneys, think carefully about your users/customers and their reasons for both needing and wanting your product.
- Focusing realistically will help you target realistically and tell your story most powerfully and effectively.
- Appealing not only to investors but also to philanthropists might give you a lucrative additional source of funding.
- If at first you don't succeed, go back to the drawing board and imagine another path to your goal.

AUTHOR'S AFTERWORD

AN ALPHABET OF EXPECTATIONS

THE JURY IS STILL OUT on a number of my projects. Certainly none of that slows me down, but sometimes I can't help but feel like I have a permanent seat on one of those benches located just outside the courtroom. As of this writing, we are waiting for the National Institutes of Health (NIH) to sign off on a grant at Inverseon. Inverseon and a potential partner, a public company in Australia, have also announced a merger which must be approved by shareholders in the next couple of months. With regard to the Innovation Angel Card, we have applied for not for profit status with the IRS and await approval. Meanwhile, Capital One Financial Corp. (NYSE: COF) recently agreed to issue the Card — a most exciting and encouraging development! At the same time, we are strategizing DelMar's next interaction with the Food and Drug Administration (FDA).

The JOBS bill was just signed into law, hopefully making access to capital a bit easier for startups and small companies as they go forward.

Meanwhile, the "other shoe" has yet to fall, and every day is filled with ambiguity. No problem: change is the only constant in the start-up life. Well, except for pushing the limits of bureaucracy, not to mention the need for patience.

If this is the life you have also chosen, I hope this book, in addition to giving you some helpful advice and ideas to consider, also lets you know you are far from alone, even on your darker days. We've all been there, and we all came back — sometimes frustrated and empty-handed but, more often than not, triumphant. So my suggestion is — do as I do and embrace the *journey*!

One last word to investors: If one of our EGB projects strikes a chord with you, or you want help with finding and managing an intellectual property you can get behind, let's be in touch. And entrepreneurs, if you have a venture you want to get off the ground and want advice on funding it, please let me know how I may be of assistance to you.

Thank you for sharing this time with me, and best of luck!

BILL GARNER

San Francisco, CA
www.egbadvisors.com

ABOUT THE AUTHOR

WILLIAM J. ("BILL") GARNER, MD, MPH, founded EGB Advisors in 2000, originally to serve as a pharmaceutical licensing boutique. Early EGB clients included the MD Anderson Cancer Center Office of Technology Commercialization, the Kauffman Foundation, CoTherix and ChemGenex.

Prior to EGB, Bill worked in medical affairs in oncology at Hoffmann-LaRoche. Before that he was an associate in a merchant bank on Wall Street. He was also the co-founder and CEO of an online business-to-business company for management of capital equipment used in drug discovery, research and clinical laboratories.

Beginning in 2004, with proceeds from the sale of equity stakes in client companies, Bill began to develop drug companies, each with the potential to shift treatment paradigms. These include Inverseon, developing a novel therapy for smoking cessation, chronic cough and COPD; and Urigen Pharmaceuticals, developing a drug which is instilled in the bladder for Interstitial Cystitis. As CEO, Bill took Urigen public, and the company's lead product achieved statistical significance on all endpoints in a placebo-controlled, double-blind, multi-center trial. Bill also catalyzed the founding of an oncology company, bringing the other executives together to form DelMar Pharmaceuticals. DelMar is now modernizing an oncology drug that was originally studied in numerous phase II clinical trials in the U.S. in the 1980s and has been successfully commercialized in parts of China.

Bill is an inventor with multiple patent filings. He is also incubating

Innovation Angel Card to combine a credit card affinity program with grants to innovative companies.

Bill earned a BA, cum laude, in Sociology from Texas Christian University, a Master of Public Health from Harvard, and his MD degree from New York Medical College. He did residency training in anatomic pathology at Columbia-Presbyterian and is a licensed physician in the State of New York. During his medical career, Bill has been honored with several awards, including the American Medical Association/Wellcome Resident Physician Leadership Award, an annual leadership and community service award given to only 40 physicians nationwide. He has lectured on entrepreneurship at Case Western Reserve University and is a member of the Board of Directors of ImmunoGenetix in Kansas City.

Made in the USA
Charleston, SC
14 December 2012